The Sadistically Delicious Series

Air Fryer Cookbook

101 Simple and Delicious Air Fryer Recipes for Fantastic Food Fast

Evelyn Halliday

Contents

Introduction

Welcome to the first book in **The Sadistically Delicious Series** of creative recipe books, *Air Fryer Cookbook, 101 Simple and Delicious air Fryer Recipes for Fantastic Food Fast.* I would like to thank you for choosing this book to aid in your journey to becoming a culinary mastermind. The Sadistically Delicious Series was designed with the goal of helping others get professional results from their home kitchen appliances every time. This book, the first in the series is dedicated to Air Fryer cooking, keep your eyes peeled for the second book in the series **Pressure Cooker Cookbook** coming soon.

This book , *Air Fryer Cookbook, 101 Simple and Delicious air Fryer Recipes for Fantastic Food Fast* was written with the aim of helping others to get the most out of their Air Fryers. The recipes contained within have been creatively designed to complement each other and fully utilise the different styles and techniques involve with cooking by air fryer. Air Fryers have the rare ability of being able to create healthy option meals without sacrificing flavour. Being easy to use, clean and maintain makes the air fryer a must for any modern kitchen owner. Beyond just frying these sleek kitchen gadgets also grill, roast and even bake!

A few of the other benefits of Air Fryer cooking are:

- Healthier than deep or shallow fried food

- Food is cooked quickly and evenly

- Small sleek designs allow for easy storage.

- Automatic shutdown features stop food from burning

I hope you enjoy and are inspired by the recipes within.

Best wishes

Evelyn Halliday

Recommended Air Fryers

Philips HD9220/26 Healthier Oil Free Airfryer

The **Philips HD9220/26 Healthier Oil Free Airfryer** is a fantastic bit of kit and includes **adjustable temperature and timer dials** making changes to settings easy. The temperature can be set up to 390°f and the timer can be set up to 30 minutes.

Like other Philips Air fryers the **Philips HD9220/26 Viva Collection Digital Airfryer** utilises **Rapid Air Technology** which circulates hot air throughout the air fryer in order to evenly cook food.

The multi-faceted nature of the **Philips HD9220/26 Healthier Oil Free Airfryer** is not limited to frying but also bakes, grills and roasts.

Philips HD9240/94 Avance Collection Airfryer

The **Philips HD9240/94 Avance Collection Airfryer** includes a **Digital Touchscreen Interface** which allows for quick and easy adjustments to be made to the air fryer.

This model provides a large **detachable cooking basket** which is easy to clean and has a huge cooking capacity.

The **Smart pre-set button** will remember the settings for your favourite dishes so that they can be recalled in the future at the touch of a button.

Philips HD9230/26 Viva Collection Digital Airfryer

The **Digital Touchscreen Interface** allows for quick and easy adjustments to be made to the air fryer.

The **Double Layer Rack** provides a larger cooking surface and the huge 1.8lb basket allows for a greater cooking capacity.

The clever and stylish **Design** of this air fryer means although it has a large cooking capacity it is extremely compact and the **Non-slip Feet** ensure maximum safety.

GoWISE GW22631 Air Fryer

The **GoWise GW22631 Air fryer** is a superb air fryer with **7 Smart modes** and 4 cooking styles, frying, roasting, baking and grilling. This easy to clean model has a non-stick food basket (slightly smaller than the Philips models) and a fantastic design.

Duronic AF1 Healthy Oil Free multi-cooker fryer

The **Duronic AF1** is a healthier way to cook your food without compromising on flavour. This model is dishwasher safe and runs at 1500W and uses little or no oil when cooking.

The **Duronic AF1 Healthy Oil Free multi-cooker fryer** is the Cheapest of the air fryers mentioned.

Appetisers

World Class Buffalo Wings

Ingredients

2 Pounds of Chicken Wings

1 Cup of Hot Sauce (see below)

Salt and Ground Black Pepper for seasoning

Ingredients (Hot Sauce)

2 Tablespoons of Olive Oil

1 Cup of finely chopped Onion

2 Medium heat Chili Peppers finely chopped

3 Habanero Chili Peppers halved, seeded and finely chopped

3 Cloves of Garlic finely chopped

3 Cups of diced Tomatoes

½ Cup distilled White Vinegar

2 Teaspoons of Salt

3 Teaspoons of Sugar

Method

Start by making Hot Sauce

1. Heat the olive oil in a saucepan over a medium-high heat. Add the Onions, Garlic, Chili Peppers and Habaneros to suit your taste. Cook for 4 minutes or until the Onions start to brown, stir throughout.

2. Lower the hob to medium heat and add the Tomatoes, Vinegar, Salt, Pepper and Sugar to suit your taste. Cook for 4 minutes until the tomatoes break down, stir throughout.

3. Pour the sauce from the hob to a blender and puree until smooth.

4. Pour the blended sauce through a sieve in to a bowl and leave to cool.

Preparing your Buffalo Wings

1. Ready the Chicken wings by separating the wingtips.

2. Separate the drummettes and winglets and place in a bowl add Salt and Pepper for seasoning.

3. Pour the Hot Sauce over the Chicken and stir, ensure the Chicken is properly coated- marinade for a minimum of 3 hours.

Cooking your Buffalo Wings

1. Pre-heat the air fryer to 400°f.

2. Air fry the chicken for 15 minutes, shake midway.

Serving

Cover the Buffalo Wings in the remainder of the Hot Sauce and serve.

Bread Rolls

Ingredients

500g Bread Flour

110g Unsalted Butter

60g Sugar

2 Eggs

1 Cup of Milk (room temperature)

2 Teaspoons of Activated Yeast

1 ½ Teaspoons of Salt

Olive Oil

Method

1. In a large bowl mix the Flour, Butter, Eggs, Salt, Milk and Activated Yeast.

2. Knead your bread mix for up to 20 minutes and leave in a safe warm place for 1 to 1 ½ hours.

3. Once the dough has risen, brake away small handfuls of the dough and form rolls or bun shapes.

4. Lightly spray with Olive Oil before cooking.

Cooking your Bread Rolls

1. Pre-heat your air fryer to 340°f.

2. Place the Bread Rolls into the air fryer either 4 or 6 at a time and cook for 13-17 minutes depending on how crispy you like your Bread Rolls. Do not stack the rolls when cooking.

Serving

Serve hot with Butter.

Salmon Cakes

Ingredients

1 Large tin of Salmon, properly drained

2 Eggs lightly beaten

1 Cup of Breadcrumbs

2 Tablespoons of Olive Oil

Salt and Ground Black Pepper to taste

½ Teaspoon of Cayenne Pepper

2 Tablespoons of finely chopped fresh Parsley

Method

1. Using a fork mash together the Salmon, Eggs, Parsley, Cayenne Pepper along with a little Salt and Pepper to taste.

2. Mix the Breadcrumbs and Olive Oil together

3. Shape the Salmon mix into 14 mini Salmon Cakes and thoroughly coat them in the Breadcrumb and Olive Oil mix.

Cooking your Salmon Cakes

1. Pre-heat your air fryer to 390°f.

2. Cook the Salmon Cakes for 7 minutes turning midway.

Serving

Serve with a Mixed Salad.

Cayenne Crabsticks

Ingredients

1 Packet of Crabsticks

½ Teaspoon Cayenne Pepper

1 Tablespoon of Olive Oil

Salt to taste

Method

1. Mix the Olive Oil, Cayenne Pepper and a little Salt to taste in a bowl.

2. Place the Crabsticks into the Olive Oil and Cayenne mix and make sure they are fully coated. Let any excess mix drip back into the bowl.

Cooking your Cayenne Crabsticks

1. Pre-heat your air fryer to 340°f.

2. Air fry your Crabsticks for 10 minutes tossing regularly to ensure they are cooking evenly.

Serving

Serve hot or cold.

French Toast Soldiers

Ingredients

2 Day old Bread

2 Eggs lightly beaten

Butter

Olive Oil

Salt and Ground Black Pepper to taste

Method

1. Butter the Bread and cut horizontally in half and cut the halves into strips.

2. Add a little Salt and Ground Pepper to the beaten Eggs to taste.

3. Put the Bread into the Egg mix, fully submerging the Bread ensuring it is fully covered.

Cooking your French Toast Soldiers

1. Pre-heat your air fryer to 380°f.

2. Arrange the Bread sticks in the air fryer and cook for 2 minutes before lightly spraying the bread with Olive Oil and turning. Cook for a further 4 minutes checking regularly.

Serving

Serve hot as a snack or as part of an English breakfast.

Risotto Balls with Chili and Tomato

Ingredients

1 Tablespoon of Olive Oil

½ An Onion, finely chopped

1 Cup of Risotto

¼ Cup White Wine

1½ Cups of Water

1 Cup Chicken Stock

Salt and Ground Black Pepper to season

2 Eggs beaten

2 Cups of Seasoned Breadcrumbs

Chili and tomato sauce

1 Red Chili, finely chopped

2 Bird's Eye Chilies, finely chopped

1 Clove of Garlic, finely chopped

1 Packet of oil packed Sun-Dried Tomatoes, chopped

1 Tablespoon of Tomato Puree

1 Teaspoon of Caster Sugar

Ground Black Pepper

Method

Start by cooking your Risotto

1. On a hob, pre-heat a large saucepan on medium heat.

2. Add the Olive Oil to the pan followed by the finely chopped Onion and sauté for 5 minutes or until the Onion has softened.

3. Pour in the Rice and stir to fully coat the Rice.

4. Add the White Wine and leave to simmer for 2 minutes.

5. Add the Chicken Stock and Water, stir well and then cover the saucepan and reduce the heat.

6. Leave on a low simmer for 20 minutes.

7. Once the Rice tender season to taste with Salt and Ground Black Pepper and stir, then spread the rice out on a baking sheet to cool.

8. When cooled add the beaten Eggs and half the Breadcrumbs to the Rice and mix thoroughly. Put the remaining Breadcrumbs into a bowl.

9. Shape the Rice mix into 12 balls and roll them in the remaining Breadcrumbs making sure they are fully covered. Place the Rice on a baking sheet and lightly spray with Olive Oil.

Cooking your Risotto Balls

1. Pre-heat your air fryer to 380°f

2. Air-fry a maximum of six Risotto Balls at a time for 8 minutes, then turn and continue to air-fry for another 8 minutes.

Whilst your Risotto Balls are cooking, prepare the Chilli and Tomato Sauce

1. Add the chopped Chillies, Garlic and Tomatoes to a saucepan, put on a low heat and stir in the Sugar, Tomato Puree and Ground Black Pepper.

2. When heated through, blend and serve.

Serving

Using a spoon, make a pool of the Chilli and Tomato Sauce on a plate, with three Risotto Balls placed in the sauce.

Ham and Cheese Puff Pastry Parcels

Ingredients

200g Ready-made Puff Pastry

Egg Wash (1 beaten egg with a little milk mixed in)

Mild Cheddar Cheese, grated

1 packed of Ham finely chopped

Method

1. Mix the chopped Ham and grated Cheddar in a bowl.

2. Cut the Puff Pastry into squares between 4cm and 6cm.

3. Place some of the mix in the middle of the Pastry squares

4. Moisten the edges of the Pastry with Egg wash and fold in half into a triangle.

5. Pinch the edges of your Pastry triangle to ensure it is properly stuck closed.

Cooking your Ham Cheese Puff Pastry Parcels

Pre-heat your air fryer to 390°f.

Cook for 10 minutes checking and tossing regularly. Cook up to 8 Ham and Cheese Puff Pastry Parcels per batch.

Fresh Tortilla Chips

Ingredients

8 Corn Tortillas

1 Tablespoon Olive Oil

Salt to taste

Method

Cut the Tortillas into triangles and brush or spray with Olive Oil.

Cooking your Tortilla Chips

1. Pre-heat your air fryer to 390°.

2. Place half the Tortilla triangles into the air fryer and cook for 2 to 3 minutes.

3. Repeat with the remaining tortilla Triangles.

Serving

Sprinkle with salt and serve hot with cheese.

Potato Crisps

Ingredients

2 Russet Burbank or Maris Piper Potatoes

Salt and Ground Pepper

Olive oil

Method

1. Slice the Potato as thinly as possible and in a uniform fashion.

2. Soak the sliced Potato for 20 minutes, changing the water midway.

3. Dry the Potato slices on a kitchen towel.

4. Spray both sides of the slices with Olive Oil and sprinkle with Salt and Ground Black Pepper.

Cooking your Potato Crisps

1. Pre-heat your air fryer to 390° for 5 minutes.

2. Toss your Potato slices into the air fryer in a haphazard manner ensure they are not stacked and cook for 22 minutes. Shake crisps regularly to ensure they are all evenly cooked.

Serving

Sprinkle with Salt and serve hot or cold.

Kale Crisps

Ingredients

1 Head of Kale

1 Tablespoon of Olive Oil

Salt to taste

1 Teaspoon Soy Sauce

Method

1. Wash and thoroughly dry the Kale.

2. Remove the Stems and tear the Kale into 2 inch pieces.

3. Mix the Kale with the Soy Sauce and Olive Oil and add a little Salt.

Cooking your Kale Crisps

1. Pre-heat your air fryer to 200°.

2. Put the Kale into the air fryer and cook for 3 minutes, tossing half way through.

Serving

Serve hot or cold with extra Salt if required.

Sweet Potato Crisps

Ingredients

2 Sweet Potatoes

Salt and Ground Pepper

Olive oil

Method

1. Slice the sweet potato as thinly as possible and in a uniform fashion.

2. Soak the sliced sweet potato for 20 minutes, changing the water midway.

3. Dry the sweet potato slices on a kitchen towel.

4. Spray both sides of the slices with olive oil and sprinkle with salt and ground pepper.

Cooking your Sweet Potato Crisps

1. Pre-heat your air fryer to 390° for 5 minutes.

2. Toss your sweet potato slices into the air fryer in a haphazard manner ensure they are not stacked and cook for 22 minutes. Shake crisps regularly to ensure they are all cooked evenly.

Serving

Sprinkle with salt and serve hot or cold.

Asian Style Cucumber Crisps

Ingredients

1 Whole Cucumber

2 Cloves of Garlic finely chopped

2 Tablespoons of Soy Sauce

½ Cup of Flour

1 Teaspoon of Paprika

2 Teaspoon of Cayenne Pepper

1 Teaspoon of Sugar

Salt and Ground Pepper to taste

1 Tablespoon of Olive Oil

Method

1. Mix the Soy Sauce, Olive Oil, Garlic, Sugar, Salt and Pepper in a bowl.

2. In a separate bowl mix the Flour, Cayenne Pepper, Paprika and a little Salt and Ground Pepper to taste.

3. Add the Cucumber slices into the soy Sauce mix and stir. Leave to marinade for 5 minutes.

4. Remove the Cucumber from the soy Sauce and throw them into the Flour mix, making sure they are full coated. Shake off any excess flour.

5. Lightly spray with Olive Oil before cooking.

Cooking your Asian Style Cucumber Crisps

1. Pre-heat your air fryer to 360°f.

2. Place the Cucumber slices in the air fryer in a haphazard fashion and cook for around 3 minutes or until crisp. Turn midway.

Serving

Serve hot with a sprinkling of Salt/Sugar mix.

Roasted Chickpeas

Ingredients

1 Tin of Chickpeas properly drained

1 Tablespoon of Olive Oil

1 Teaspoon of Mixed Spice

Method

1. Dry off your Chickpeas on some kitchen towel and throw them in a bowl along with your mixed spice and olive oil and mix.

Cooking your Roasted Chickpeas

1. Pre heat your air fryer to 390°f.

2. Cook the Chickpeas at 390°f for 8-10 minutes tossing regularly.

Serving

Serve warm in a bowl as a delicious starter or table snack.

Crispy Prawn Toast

Ingredients

500g King Prawns

2 Cloves of Garlic finely grated

2 Inch piece of Ginger finely grated

1 Onion finely chopped

1 Egg, lightly beaten and 1 Egg White

1 Teaspoon of Sesame Oil

1 Tablespoon of Olive Oil

1 Teaspoon of Caster Sugar

Panko Crumbs (found in any Asian supermarket)

Salt and Ground Pepper to taste

Sliced 2 day old Bread

Method

1. Peel and clean the King Prawns.

2. Blend the King Prawns, Garlic, Ginger, Sugar, Sesame Oil and Egg White in a food processor.

3. Once blended add the finely chopped Onion to the mix and stir well.

4. Spread a layer (approximately 2 tablespoons) of the Prawn mix on each piece of Bread and cut the bread into triangles.

5. Brush the tops of the Bread with beaten Egg.

6. Press each piece of Bread face down into the Panko Breadcrumbs ensuring they are properly coated.

7. Lightly spray your Crispy Prawn Toast with Olive Oil before cooking.

Cooking your Crispy Prawn Toast

1. Pre-heat your air fryer to 360°f.

2. Cook your Crispy Prawn Toast in batches making sure the air fryer is not overloaded.

3. Air fry your Crispy Prawn Toast for 10 minutes gently turning midway.

Serving

Serve hot with Sweet and Sour Sauce.

Crispy Vegetable Spring Rolls

Ingredients

10 Spring Roll Sheets

2 Tablespoons of Corn Flour

Water as needed

Filling

1 Carrot cut into fine strips

2 Cups shredded Cabbage

½ Red Pepper cut into fine strips

1 Onion cut into fine strips

1 Spring Onion very finely chopped

2 inch piece of Ginger very finely grated

3 Cloves of Garlic very finely grated

½ Teaspoon Sugar

Salt and freshly Ground Pepper to taste

2 Tablespoons of Olive Oil

1 Tablespoon Soy Sauce

Method

1. Add some Olive Oil to a saucepan and toss in the Cabbage, Carrots, Peppers, Onion, Spring Onion, Garlic and Ginger.

2. Add the Sugar, Salt and Ground Pepper to taste (be generous with the Ground Pepper). Sauté the vegetable for 3 minutes or until the vegetable begin to shrink.

3. Mix in the Soy Sauce add some extra Ground Pepper, mix well and remove from the heat.

Wrapping your Crispy Spring Rolls

1. Ensure your Spring Roll Sheets are properly defrosted.

2. Mix the Corn Flour and a little Water in a bowl until you have a paste.

3. Place a two inch length of the vegetable mix in the corner of your spring roll sheet and roll as shown below:

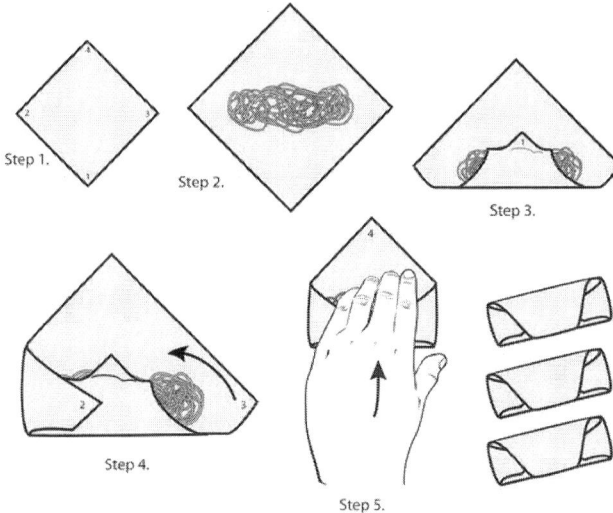

Cooking your Crispy Spring Rolls

1. Pre-heat your air fryer to 360°f and leave for 5 minutes.

2. Lightly spray the Spring Rolls with Olive Oil, place them into the air fryer and cook for 20 minutes turning at the midway point.

Serving

Serve hot or cooled.

The Ultimate Cheesy Bacon Fries

Ingredients

2 Large Russet Burbank or Maris Piper Potatoes peeled and cut into ½ inch chips/fries

4 strips of Bacon roughly chopped

1 Cup of grated mild Cheddar Cheese

3 Ounces of Mozzarella

Salt and Ground Pepper to taste

Method of Cooking the Ultimate Cheesy Bacon Fries

1. Boil a saucepan of water. Add the chopped Potatoes to the boiling water and simmer for 5 minutes.

2. Remove the Potatoes from the water, strain and dry off any excess water with kitchen towel.

3. Pre-heat your air fryer to 400°f.

4. Air fry you're the chopped Bacon for 4 minutes. Shake the frying basket mid-way to evenly cook the Bacon.

5. Remove the Bacon from the air fryer and drain any grease. Dry the Bacon off with a kitchen towel.

6. Set your air fryer to 360°f.

7. Spray the dried Potato with Olive Oil and put them into your air fryer for 22 minutes. Shake the basket every 5 minutes to

evenly cook the fries. Season the fries with Salt and Ground Pepper during the last 5 minutes.

8. Remove the fries from the air fryer and place into a small casserole dish (Make sure the dish fits inside your air fryer).

9. Mix the grated Cheddar and Mozzarella with the fries and Bacon pieces and place the casserole dish inside your air fryer.

10. Air fry at 340°f for a further 5 minutes in order to fully melt the Cheese.

Serving

Toss your Ultimate Cheesy Bacon Fries into a bowl and sprinkle on top any remaining Cheese or Bacon bits. Serve hot.

Fried Artichoke Hearts

Ingredients

8-10 Artichoke Hearts cut into halves

Olive Oil

1 Cup of Flour

½ Teaspoon of Salt

½ Teaspoon of Ground Pepper

Method

1. Mix the Flour, Salt and Pepper in a bowl.

2. Before air frying coat the Artichokes in the seasoned Flour and lightly spray with Olive Oil.

Cooking your Fried Artichoke Hearts

1. Pre-heat your air fryer to 380°f.

2. Air fry the Artichoke Hearts for 2-3 minutes or until golden brown, toss regularly.

Serving

Serve hot with Tartar Sauce and a sprinkling of Salt.

Battered Okra

Ingredients

400g Okra cut into 1 inch pieces

½ Cup of Plain Flour

2 Eggs, lightly beaten

½ Teaspoon of Paprika

½ Teaspoon Cayenne Pepper

½ Teaspoon of Salt

Method

1. Mix the Flour, Cayenne Pepper, Salt and Paprika in a bowl.

2. Put the beaten Eggs in a bowl, coat the Okra pieces in the Egg mix and let any excess drip back in the mix.

3. Coat the Okra in the Flour mix and lightly spray with Olive Oil before cooking.

Cooking your Battered Okra

1. Pre-heat your air fryer to 380°f.

2. Cook the Okra for 4-5 minutes or until golden brown.

Serving

Serve hot with hot sauce and a sprinkling of Salt.

Meat

Egg and Bacon Bakes

Ingredients

4 Large Eggs

4 Slices of Bacon

1 Handful of Cheddar Cheese grated

Salt and Ground Pepper to taste

Unsalted Butter

1 Tablespoon of Olive Oil

Method

1. Pre-heat your air-fryer to 380°f.

2. Toss the Bacon into the air fryer and cook for 6 minutes.

3. Remove the Bacon from the air fryer and chop into small pieces.

4. Remove any grease from the air fryer.

5. Coat the insides of 4 ramekins (or small oven dishes) with the unsalted butter.

6. Divide the chopped Bacon between the 4 ramekins and crack 1 Egg into each. Add a little Salt and Ground Pepper to taste and 1 teaspoon of Milk to each.

Cooking your Egg and Bacon Bakes

1. Cook at 380°f for 15 minutes and sprinkle a little cheese on top of each ramekin. Cook for a further 5 minutes or until the Egg white sets.

Serving

Serve with Toast as an ideal breakfast.

Full English Breakfast Bakes

Ingredients

4 Large Eggs

4 Hash Browns oven cooked for 10 minutes

2 Slices of Bacon cooked and chopped

2 Sausages cooked and chopped

1 Handful of Cheddar Cheese grated

Salt and Ground Pepper to taste

Unsalted Butter

1 Tablespoon of Olive Oil

Method

1. Coat the insides of 4 ramekins (or small oven dishes) with the Unsalted Butter.

2. Push 1 Hash Brown into the bottom of each ramekin.

3. Divide the chopped Bacon and Sausage pieces between the 4 ramekins.

4. Crack 1 Egg into each ramekin. Add a little Salt and Ground Pepper to taste and 1 teaspoon of Milk to each.

Cooking your Full English Breakfast Bakes

1. Pre-heat your air fryer to 380°f.

2. Cook for 15-20 minutes or until the Egg white sets.

Serving

Serve hot with a sprinkling of Cheese.

Hard Boiled Eggs on the Go

Ingredients

2-4 Medium or Large Eggs

Cooking your

1. Pre-heat your air fryer to 340°f.

2. Place the Eggs in the air fryer basket and cook for 7 minutes.

Serving

Place the Eggs in cold water and allow to cool, this makes peeling the Eggs much easier.

Coconut and Turmeric Chicken

Ingredients

3 Chicken quarters (whole leg pieces)

3 Tablespoons of Coconut Paste

2 Tablespoons of Turmeric

2 Inch piece of Ginger, grated

Salt and Ground Pepper to taste

Method

1. Minus the Chicken, mix all of the ingredients in a bowl.

2. Cut some deep slices into the Chicken pieces and then fully coat the Chicken in the mix and leave to marinade for a minimum of 2 hours to overnight.

Cooking your Coconut and Turmeric Chicken

1. Pre-heat your air fryer to 380°f.

2. Cook the Chicken pieces for 25 minutes (or until Chicken is golden brown and any juices run clear), turn midway.

Serving

Serve hot with rice.

Honey and Lime Chicken

Ingredients

4-6 Chicken Breasts

2 Cloves of Garlic finely chopped

2 Tablespoons of Honey

2 Tablespoons of freshly squeezed Lime Juice

1 Pinch of Chili Flakes

2 Tablespoons of Olive Oil

Salt and Ground Black Pepper to taste

Method

1. In a bowl mix the Hones, Olive Oil, Garlic, Lime, Chile Flakes, Salt and Ground Black Pepper to taste.

2. Cut some slices into the Chicken Breast but don't cut all the way through. Place the Chicken Breasts in the Honey and Lime mix and leave to marinade for at least 2 hours to overnight.

Cooking you Honey and Lime Chicken

1. Pre-heat your air fryer to 360°f.

2. Place your Honey and Lime Chicken Breasts into the air fryer basket and cook for 20-25 minutes or until golden brown, turning midway.

Serving

Serve hot with rice or Garlic Potatoes and Salad.

Chicken Satay Skewers

Ingredients

500g Chicken Breast, cubed

5 Tablespoons of Tomato Puree

4 Cloves of Garlic, finely chopped

¼ Onion finely chopped

1 Teaspoon of Cumin

1 Teaspoon of Ground Black Pepper

1 Tablespoons of Sesame Oil

1 Tablespoon of Peanut Oil

1 Tablespoon Soy Sauce

1 Tablespoon of Sugar

2 Tablespoons of Peanut Butter

Half a Lemon

Skewers

Method

1. Mix the Tomato Puree, Garlic, Onion, Cumin, Ground Black Pepper, Sesame Oil, Peanut Oil, Soy Sauce, Sugar, Peanut Butter, a generous squeeze of Lemon juice and a little Salt to taste.

2. Coat the Chicken pieces in the marinade and leave for a minimum of 2 hours to overnight.

3. Before cooking skewer the Chicken pieces approximately 4 pieces per skewer.

Cooking your Chicken Satay Skewers

1. Pre-heat your air fryer to 390°f.

2. Line the basket with foil and place the Chicken skewers inside.

3. Cook for 15 minutes turning midway to ensure the Chicken is evenly cooked.

Serving

Serve with Rice and a slice of Lime.

Chicken Tikka Bites

Ingredients

500g boneless Chicken, cubed.

200g Natural Yoghurt

1 Tablespoon of fresh Garlic and Ginger Paste

1 Teaspoon of Turmeric

1 Teaspoon of Chili Powder

1 Teaspoon of Cumin

1 Tablespoon of Garam Masala Mixed Spice

Salt to taste

Method

1. Pour the Natural Yoghurt into a bowl along with all of the Spices and mix thoroughly.

2. Add the Chicken cubes to the mix and mix thoroughly ensuring all the Chicken is fully coated.

3. Leave to marinade from 2 hours to overnight. Skewer the Chicken before cooking.

Cooking your Chicken Tikka Bites

1. Pre-heat your air fryer to 390°f.

2. Line the basket with foil and place the Chicken skewers inside.

3. Cook for 15 minutes turning midway to ensure the Chicken is evenly cooked.

Serving

Serve with a Rice slice of Lime.

Spicy Barbecue Drumsticks

Ingredients

500g Chicken Drumsticks

3 Gloves of Garlic finely chopped and crushed

1 Tablespoon of Brown Sugar

1 Teaspoon of Paprika

½ Teaspoon of Cumin

½ Teaspoon of Mustard Powder

1 Tablespoon of Olive Oil

1 Tablespoon of White Wine Vinegar

2 Tablespoons of Golden Syrup

3 Tablespoons of Barbecue Sauce

Methods

1. Mix all of the ingredients together in a bowl and then mix in the Chicken ensuring all the Drumsticks are evenly covered.

2. Leave to marinade from a minimum of 2 hours but preferably overnight.

Cooking your Spicy Barbecue Drumsticks

1. Pre heat your air fryer to 390°f.

2. Cook the Chicken Drumsticks for 10 minutes at 390° and turn. After turning continue cooking 300°f for a further 10 minutes or until caramelised and crisp.

Serving

Serve hot with Fries or Wedges.

Dry Rub Chicken Bites

Ingredients

500g boneless Chicken, cubed.

1 Teaspoon Garlic Powder

1 Teaspoon Ginger powder

½ Teaspoon Cumin

½ Teaspoon Fresh Ground pepper

Salt to taste

Method

1. Mix the spices together in a bowl.

2. Generously apply an even coating of the dry rub mix to the Chicken.

Cooking your Dry Rub Chicken Bites

1. Pre-heat your air fryer to 390°f.

2. Line the basket with foil and place the Chicken skewers inside.

3. Cook for 15 minutes turning midway to ensure the Chicken is evenly cooked.

Serving

Serve hot with Rice, Fries or Wedges.

World Class Chicken Nuggets

Ingredients

500g Boneless Chicken, cubed

2 Eggs, beaten

2 Cups of Flour

½ Teaspoon of Paprika

½ Teaspoon of Ground Black Pepper

Salt to taste

Olive Oil

Method

1. Mix the Flour, Black Pepper, Paprika, Salt and Ground Black Pepper in a bowl. Then add the Egg and mix thoroughly.

2. Add the Chicken to the batter mix ensuring it is fully and evenly covered.

Cooking your World Class Chicken Nuggets

1. Line your air fryer basket with foil and pre-heat the air fryer to 380°f.

2. Give your Nuggets a light spraying of Olive Oil before tossing them into the air fryer.

3. Cook for 18-20 minutes tossing regularly.

Serving

Serve with dips, Ketchup, Barbecue and Hot Sauce.

Lebanese Chicken

Ingredients

4-6 Chicken Quarters

2 Tablespoons of Natural Yoghurt

2 Tablespoons of Tomato Puree

2 Cloves of Garlic finely chopped

1 Tablespoon of Mustard

1 Tablespoon of Ground Allspice

1 Teaspoon of Paprika

½ Teaspoon Cinnamon

½ Teaspoon of Ground Black Pepper

1 Teaspoon of Curry Powder

Method

1. Mix the Yoghurt, Tomato Puree, Garlic, Mustard, Allspice, Paprika, Cinnamon, Ground Black Pepper, Curry Powder and a little Salt to taste and mix well.

2. Coat the Chicken quarters in the marinade and leave for at least 2 hours up to overnight.

Cooking your Lebanese Chicken

1. Pre-heat your air fryer to 380°f.

2. Cook the Chicken Quarters for 20-25 minutes or until golden brown and any juices run clear. Be sure not to overload the air fryer.

Serving

Serve hot with Rice and a slice of Lime.

Air Fried Pigs in Blankets

Ingredients

16 Mini Sausages

1 Pack of Bacon

Olive Oil

Method

1. Cut the Bacon into 2 inch strips, enough for 1 strip per Sausage.

2. Wrap the Bacon strips tightly around the Sausages.

Cooking your Air Fried Pigs in Blankets

1. Pre-heat your air fryer to 380°f.

2. Cook the Pigs in Blankets for 20 minutes.

Serving

Serve hot, perfect with a roast dinner.

Pork, Sage and Onion Stuffing Balls

Ingredients

100g Sausage Meat

½ Onion very finely chopped

1 Teaspoon Sage

½ Teaspoon of Garlic Puree

Salt and Ground Black Pepper to taste

½ cup of Breadcrumbs

Method

1. Throw all of your ingredients into a bowl and mix very well.

2. Using your hands roll the mix into small to medium sized ball and lightly spray with Olive Oil.

Cooking your Pork, Sage and Onion Stuffing Balls

1. Pre-heat your air fryer to 390°f.

2. Place the Stuffing Balls into the air fryer for 18 minutes tossing midway.

Serving

Serve with Chicken, Mixed Vegetables and gravy.

Sweet and Spicy Chicken Wings

Ingredients

500g Chicken Wings

2 Cloves of Garlic

1 Teaspoon of Ginger Powder

½ Teaspoon of Cumin

1 Teaspoon of Paprika

1 Tablespoon of Golden Syrup

1 Teaspoon of Brown Sugar

½ Teaspoon of fresh Ground pepper

2 Tablespoons of Olive Oil

Salt to taste

Method

1. Mix all the ingredients together in a bowl.
2. Mix in the Chicken Wings ensuring they are properly and evenly covered.

Cooking your Sweet and Spicy Chicken Wings

1. Pre-heat your air fryer to 390°f
2. Cook for 12 minutes turning midway to ensure the chicken is evenly cooked.

Serving

Serve hot with Rice, Fries or Wedges.

Tandoori Chicken Quarters

Ingredients

2-4 Chicken Quarters

1½ Teaspoons of Tandoori paste

1 Teaspoon of Garlic Paste

1 Teaspoon of Ginger Paste

½ Tablespoon of Lemon Juice

Salt and ground Black Pepper to taste

Method

1. Mix the Tandoori Paste, Garlic Paste, Ginger Paste, Lemon Juice and a little Salt and Ground Black Pepper to taste.

2. Coat the Chicken Quarters in the Tandoori Paste mix and leave to marinade for at least 2 hours to overnight.

3. Lightly spray the marinated Chicken Quarters with Olive Oil before cooking.

Cooking your Tandoori Chicken Quarters

1. Pre heat your air fryer to 360°f.

2. Carefully place your Tandoori Chicken Quarters in the air fryer basket and cook for 20-25 minutes or until golden brown and beginning to crisp.

Serving

Serve with Garlic Seasoned Potatoes.

Spicy Indian Style Chicken Breast

Ingredients

4-6 Chicken Breasts

½ Cup of Natural Yoghurt

1 Teaspoon of Turmeric

½ Teaspoon of Paprika

½ Teaspoon of Cumin

½ Garlic Powder

½ Teaspoon of Chili Powder

1 Teaspoon of Garam Masala

Salt and Ground Black Pepper to taste

Method

1. Mix the Yoghurt, Turmeric, Paprika, Cumin, Garam Masala, Garlic powder, Chili Power and a little Salt and Pepper to taste.
2. Cut slices into the chicken breasts but do not cut them all the way through.
3. Coat the Chicken in the marinade mix and leave them to marinade for a minimum of 3 hours to overnight.

Cooking your Spicy Indian Style Chicken Breast

1. Pre-heat your air fryer to 380°f.
2. Place the Spicy Indian Chicken Breast in the baking tray and into the air fryer and cook for 20-25 minutes turning midway.

Serving

Serve hot with Rice and a slice of Lemon.

Sweet and Sticky Pork

Ingredients

4 Pork Loins

1 Cloves of Garlic finely chopped

1 inch piece of Ginger, grated

2 Tablespoons of Honey

1 Tablespoon of Soy Sauce

¼ Teaspoon fresh Ground Black Pepper

¼ Teaspoon mild Chili Powder

1 Teaspoon of Balsamic Vinegar

1 Tablespoon of Olive Oil

Method

1. Mix all of the spices (half the Ground Black Pepper), Honey, Olive Oil and Soy Sauce in a bowl.
2. Tenderise the Pork Loins, season with the ground Pepper and cut them into strips.
3. Add the Pork Loin strips to the mix and fully cover.
4. Leave to marinade for a minimum of 2 hours up to overnight.

Cooking your Sweet and Sticky Pork

1. Pre-heat your air fryer to 360°f.
2. Place the Pork Loin strips along with the marinade into the baking tray and air fry/air bake for 8 minutes on each side or until golden brown.

Serving

Serve hot with Fries or Wedges.

Mini Roasted Duck Pies

Ingredients

350g Roasted Duck shredded and finely chopped

½ Red Onion very finely chopped

2 Tablespoons of Hoisin Sauce

Salt and Ground Black Pepper to taste

Olive Oil

Gow Gee Wrappings

Garnish

Spring Onions thinly sliced

Cucumber Slices

Plum Sauce

Method

1. Mix the Duck, Onion and Hoisin Sauce and add Salt and Ground Black Pepper to season.

2. Encase some of the mix between 2 gow gee wrappings.

3. Repeat the process for the remainder of the Duck, Onion and Hoisin mix.

4. Lightly spray your mini Roasted Duck Pies with Olive Oil.

Cooking your Mini Roasted Duck Pies

1. Pre-heat your air fryer to 380°f.

2. Air fry your mini Roasted Duck Pies in batches, be sure not to overload your air fryer.

3. Air fry your mini Roasted Duck Pies for 12-14 minutes turning midway.

Serving

Serve hot with Plum Sauce, Cucumber slices and Spring Onion garnish.

Air Fried Steak and Asparagus

Ingredients

Sirloin or Fillet Steaks

125g Asparagus

Olive Oil

Salt and Ground Black Pepper to taste

1 Teaspoon of Butter

Method

1. Season the Steaks with Salt and Ground Black Pepper and lightly spray with Olive Oil.

2. Season the Asparagus with Salt and Ground Black Pepper and lightly spray with Olive Oil, put to one side.

Cooking your Air Fried Steak and Asparagus

1. Pre-heat your air fryer to 380°f for 5 minutes.

2. Place your Steaks onto the air fryer baking tray and cook for 6 minutes before turning and cooking for a further 3 minutes. When the Steaks have been cooking for 4 minutes, toss the Asparagus into the air fryer with the Steak.

Serving

Serve hot with Salad and a little salt and Butter for the Asparagus.

Air Fried Beef Burgers

Ingredients

300g Minced Beef

1 Onion very finely chopped

1 Clove of Garlic very finely chopped

1 Teaspoon of Horseradish Sauce

1 Heaped teaspoon of Tomato Puree

1 Teaspoon of Mixed Herbs

Salt and Ground Pepper to taste

Method

1. Thoroughly mix all of the ingredients in a bowl and leave to rest in the fridge for 30 minutes.

2. Remove from the fridge and, using your hands shape the mix into 4 Burgers.

Cooking you Air Fried Beef Burgers

1. Pre-heat your air fryer to 380°f.

2. Lightly spray the Burgers with Olive Oil and place in the air fryer.

3. Cook for 20 minutes, turn the Burgers and cook for a further 15 minutes checking regularly.

Serving

Serve with Bread Rolls, Salad, Mustard and Ketchup.

Spam Fritters

Ingredients

1 Tin of Spam, sliced

2 Eggs beaten

1 Cup of Flour

1 Teaspoon of Cayenne Pepper

½ teaspoon of Baking Powder

Salt to taste

Method

1. Mix the Flour, Eggs, Cayenne Pepper, Baking Powder and a little Salt to taste and whisk until smooth.

2. Dip and fully cover the Spam slices in the batter, allowing any excess batter to drip back into the mix.

3. Lightly spray the fritters with Olive Oil before air frying.

Cooking your Spam Fritters

1. Pre-heat your air fryer to 380°f.

2. Cook your Spam fritter for 12-15 minutes turning midway.

Serving

Serve hot with Salad and Fries.

Lamb and Bulgur Shish

Ingredients

400g Lean Minced Lamb

¾ Cup of Bulgur Wheat

1 Red Onion finely chopped

1 Small handful of fresh Coriander Leaves chopped

¼ Teaspoon of Ground Allspice

½ Teaspoon of Cumin

½ Teaspoon of Medium Heat Chili Power

Salt and Ground Black Pepper to taste

Olive Oil

Skewers

Method

1. Add 2 cups of water to a medium saucepan along with the Bulgur Wheat and bring to the boil before removing from the heat. Put a lid on the pan and leave for 10-12 minutes before pouring out any excess water.

2. To the Bulgur Wheat, add the Coriander Leaves, Allspice, Chili Powder, Onion, Minced Lamb and Salt and Ground Black Pepper to taste.

3. Using your hands shape the Lamb mix into cylinders (10-14) and skewer each vertically.

4. Lightly spray each lamb skewer before cooking.

Cooking your Lamb and Bulgur Shish

1. Pre-heat your air fryer to 380°f.

2. Air fry the Lamb and Bulgur Shish skewers for 18-22 minutes or until golden brown turning midway.

Serving

Serve hot with Pitta Bread, Lettuce and grated Carrot.

Air Fried Gammon and Pineapple

Ingredients

Gammon Steaks

Pineapples rings 1 per Gammon Steak

Salt and Ground Pepper to taste

1 Tablespoon of Olive Oil

¼ Teaspoon Cayenne Pepper

Method

1. Mix the Honey, Olive Oil, Cayenne pepper a little Salt and ground Black Pepper to taste.

2. Coat the Gammon Steaks before Cooking.

Cooking your Air Fried Gammon and Pineapple

1. Pre-heat your air fryer to 380°f.

2. Air fry the Gammon Steaks for 10-12 minutes or until golden brown, turning midway.

Fish

Everyone's Favourite Battered Cod

Ingredients

2-4 Cod Loin Fillets

1 Cup of Flour

2 Egg Whites

½ Teaspoon of Baking Soda

½ Teaspoon of Paprika

½ Teaspoon of Salt

½ Teaspoon of Fresh Ground Black Pepper

1 Cup of 2 day old Breadcrumbs

Method

1. Start by mixing together the Flour, Baking Soda, Paprika, Salt and fresh Ground Black Pepper.

2. Add the beaten Egg and whisk until the mixture is smooth.

3. Put the Breadcrumbs in a separate bowl.

4. Dip the Cod Fillets in the batter mix ensuring both sides are properly covered. Allow any excess batter to rip back into the mix.

5. Next, place the Cod Fillets in the Breadcrumbs ensuring both sides are properly covered. Use your hands to press both sides of the Cod Fillets to ensure the Breadcrumbs are stuck fast.

Cooking Everyone's Favourite Battered Cod

1. Pre-heat the air fryer to 380°f.

2. Place the Cod Loins into the air fryer and cook for 12-15 minutes or until golden brown.

Serving

Serve hot with Fries, Salt, Malt Vinegar and a slice of Lemon.

Beer Batter Cod

Ingredients

2-4 Cod Fillets cleaned and deshelled.

1 Cup of Flour

¼ Teaspoon of Baking Soda

½ Teaspoon of Paprika

1 Teaspoon of Salt

½ Teaspoon of Fresh Ground Black Pepper

½ Cup of Beer

Method

1. Start by mixing together the Flour, Baking Soda, Paprika, Salt, Pepper and Beer in a bowl.

2. Whisk until the mixture is smooth.

3. Dip the Cod Fillets in the Beer Batter, ensuring they are properly coated. Allow any excess batter to drip back into the mix.

Cooking your Beer Batter Cod

1. Line the bottom of your air fryer with foil and pre-heat your air fryer to 380°f.

2. Cook the Beer Battered Cod for 10-12 minutes or until golden brown, turning midway

Serving

Serve hot with Fries, Salt, Malt Vinegar and squeeze of Lemon.

Breaded Cajun Cod

Ingredients

2-4 Cod Loin Fillets

1 ½ Tablespoons of Cajun Seasoning

½ A Cup Flour

1 Cup of 2 day old Bread, Breadcrumbs

2 Egg Whites

2 Tablespoons of Milk

Salt and Ground Black Pepper to taste

Method

1. Mix the Flour, Cajun Seasoning and Breadcrumbs with a little Salt and Ground Black Pepper to taste.

2. Add the Egg Whites and Milk to the mix and whisk until smooth.

3. Dip the Cod Loins into the mix and ensure they are evenly covered, allow any excess mix to drip back into the bowl.

Cooking your Breaded Cajun Cod

1. Place the baking tray into the air fryer and pre-heat your air fryer to 380°f.

2. Place the Breaded Cajun Cod into the air fryer and cook for 12-15 minutes.

Serving

Serve with Fries, Salt, Malt Vinegar and a squeeze of Lime.

Lemonade Fish Fingers

Ingredients

2 Large Cod Fillets without skin, cut into even slices.

180ml Lemonade

100g Flour

1 Teaspoon of Cayenne Pepper

Salt to taste

Olive Oil

Method

1. Mix the Flour, Cayenne Pepper and Salt and add the Lemonade whilst whisking continuously until you have a smooth mixture.

2. Dip the Cod pieces into the batter and let any excess batter drip back into the mix.

Cooking your Lemonade Fish Fingers

1. Line the air fryer's basket with foil and pre-heat your air fryer to 380°f.

2. Lightly spray with Olive Oil and place the Lemonade Fish Fingers into the basket and air fry for 12-14 minutes turning midway.

Serving

Serve hot with Fries, Salt, Malt Vinegar and a slice of Lemon.

Soy Sauce Cod with Apple, Fennel and Dill

Ingredients

4 Cod Fillets

1 Clove of Garlic finely chopped

½ Teaspoon of Ground Fennel Seeds

½ Teaspoon of Dried Dill

2 Tablespoons of Soy Sauce

2 Tablespoons of Sesame Oil

Salt and Ground Black Pepper to taste

4 Sprigs of Fresh Dill finely chopped

1 Fennel Bulb sliced

1 Apple, sliced.

Method

1. Mix the Garlic, Ground Fennel Seeds, Dried Dill, Soy Sauce, 1 tablespoon of Sesame Oil.

2. Season the Cod with Salt and Ground Black Pepper and place the Cod in the marinade for a minimum of 30 minutes up to 2 hours.

Garnish

1. In a separate bowl mix the sliced Apple, Fennel, chopped Dill, 1 tablespoon of Sesame Oil and a little Salt and ground Black Pepper to taste.

Cooking your Soy Sauce Cod with Apple, Fennel and Dill

1. Put the baking tray into your air fryer and pre-heat your air fryer to 380°f.

2. Place the marinate Cod Fillets in the air fryer and cook for 8-12 minutes or until they are golden brown.

Serving

Serve hot with the sliced Apple, Fennel and Dill garnish.

Thai Style Haddock

Ingredients

2-4 Haddock Fillets

1 Inch piece of Ginger grated

2 Lemongrass stalks chopped

1 White Onion finely chopped

2 Red Chilies seeded and chopped

1 Teaspoon of Coriander

1 Teaspoon of Crushed Peppercorns

2 Kaffir Lime Leaves chopped

1 Tablespoon Sesame Oil

Salt and Ground Pepper to taste

Method

1. In a bowl, mix the Ginger, Lemongrass Stalks, Onion, Chillies, Coriander, Crushed Peppercorns, Lime Leaves, Sesame Oil and a little Salt and Ground Black Pepper to taste.

2. Place the Haddock in the mix, fully cover and leave to marinade for a minimum of 3 hours.

Cooking your Thai Style Haddock

1. Take the Haddock out of the marinade and pour the marinade into the baking tray, place the haddock on top of the marinade mix and cook for 10 minutes turning midway.

Serving

Serve with Rice, Fries or Salad.

Smoked Haddock Fritters

Ingredients

2 Smoked Haddock Fillets, skinned and shredded

2 Medium Russet Burbank or Maris Piper Potatoes peeled and halved

1 Teaspoon of Chives

1 Large tablespoon of Horseradish Sauce

1 Teaspoon of Butter

2 Eggs, well beaten

1 ½ cups of Seasoned Breadcrumbs

Salt and Ground Black Pepper to taste

Method

1. Boil the Potatoes in a medium saucepan for 18 minutes. Melt the Butter in the microwave whilst the Potatoes boil.

2. Drain the Potatoes and mash them along with the Olive Oil, Butter and some Salt and Ground Black Pepper to taste. Leave to cool.

3. Shred the Haddock and mix thoroughly into the Mashed Potato along with the Chives, Horseradish Sauce, Butter and a little Salt and Ground Black Pepper to taste.

4. Using your hands form Croquette shapes from the Fritter mixture.

5. Coat the Fritters in the Egg wash and evenly cover in Seasoned Breadcrumbs. Pat the Breadcrumbs down to ensure they are properly stuck.

Cooking your Smoked Haddock Fritters

1. Pre-heat your air fryer to 380°f.

2. Cook your Smoked Haddock fritters for 12-14 minutes or until golden brown, turning midway.

Serving

Serve hot with Salad.

Tandoori Salmon Steaks

Ingredients

2-4 Salmon Steaks

1½ Teaspoons of Tandoori Paste

1 Teaspoon of Garlic Paste

1 Teaspoon of Ginger Paste

½ Tablespoon of Lemon Juice

Salt and Ground Black Pepper to taste

Method

1. Mix the Tandoori Paste, Garlic Paste, Ginger Paste, Lemon juice and a little Salt and Pepper to taste.

2. Coat the Salmon Steaks in the Tandoori Paste mix and leave to marinade for 2 hours to overnight.

3. Lightly spray the marinated Salmon Steaks with Olive Oil before cooking.

Cooking your Tandoori Salmon Steaks

1. Pre heat your air fryer to 360°f.

2. Carefully place your Tandoori Salmon Steaks in the air fryer basket and cook for 15-18 minutes or until golden brown and beginning to crisp.

Serving

Serve with Garlic Seasoned Potatoes.

Seared Mackerel with Ginger, Coriander and Spring Onions

Ingredients

4 Mackerel Fillets, deboned

2 Red Chilies seeded and finely chopped

1 Inch piece of Ginger, grated

1 Clove of Garlic finely grated

½ Teaspoon of Dried Coriander

1 Handful of Spring Onions chopped

Half a Lime

2 Tablespoons of Olive Oil

Salt and Ground Black Pepper to taste

Method

1. Mix the Chilies, Ginger, Garlic, Dried Coriander, Olive Oil, a generous squeeze of Lime and Salt and Ground Black Pepper to taste, in a bowl.

2. Place the Mackerel in the marinade and leave for at least 2 hours.

Cooking your Seared Mackerel with Ginger, Coriander and Spring Onions

1. Place the baking tray into your air fryer and pre heat your air fryer to 380°f.

2. Cook the Mackerel Fillets for 6 minutes turning midway.

Serving

Serve hot with a sprinkling of Spring Onion and a squeeze of Lime.

Lemony Garlic Prawns

Ingredients

500g Prawns peeled and cleaned

2 Cloves of Garlic finely chopped

Half a Lemon

Salt and Ground Black Pepper to taste

1 Tablespoon of Olive Oil

Cooking your Lemony Garlic Prawns

1. Pre-heat the air fryer to 390°f.

2. Mix the Olive Oil and Garlic and pour into the air fryer.

3. Toss the Prawns into the air fryer along with a couple squeezes of Lemon juice and Salt and Pepper.

4. Cook for 8 minutes tossing regularly.

Serving

Serve hot as a starter or with Rice as a main.

Beer Batter Prawns

Ingredients

500g Prawns, cleaned and deshelled.

1 Cup of Flour

¼ Teaspoon of Baking Soda

½ Teaspoon of Paprika

1 Teaspoon of Salt

½ Teaspoon of Fresh Ground Black Pepper

½ Cup of Beer

Method

1. Start by mixing together the Flour, Baking Soda, Paprika, Salt, Pepper and Beer in a bowl.

2. Whisk until the mixture is smooth.

3. Dip the Prawns in the Beer batter ensuring they are properly coated.

Cooking your Beer Batter Prawns

1. Line the bottom of your air fryer with foil and pre-heat your air fryer to 360°f.

2. Cook the Beer Battered Prawns for 6 minutes or until golden brown.

Serving

Serve hot with a squeeze of Lemon.

Seabass Cajun Style

Ingredients

4-6 Seabass Fillets

1 Teaspoon of Cayenne Pepper

1 Teaspoon of Paprika

½ Teaspoon of Dried Oregano

½ Teaspoon of Garlic powder

½ Teaspoon of dried Thyme

Olive Oil

Salt and Ground Black Pepper to taste

Method

1. Mix all of the herbs and spices in a bowl.

2. Place the Seabass fillets into the mix, turning to ensure both sides are properly covered.

3. Lightly spray the seasoned sea bass fillets with olive oil.

Cooking your Seabass Cajun Style

1. Pre-heat your air fryer to 380°.

2. Cook for 8-10 minutes or until the fillets begin to crisp.

Serving

Serve with Salad or Rice.

Lemon and Lime Seabass

Ingredients

4-6 Seabass Fillets

2 Cloves of Garlic finely chopped

½ A Lemon

½ A Lime

¼ Teaspoon of Dried Basil

¼ Teaspoon of Dried Oregano

Salt and Ground Black Pepper to taste

1 Tablespoon of Olive Oil

Method

1. Mix the Herbs, Garlic, Lemon, Lime and Olive Oil in a bowl.

2. Place the Seabass Fillets in the mix and leave to marinade for 20 minutes.

3. When removing the seabass from the marinade ensure the excess marinade drips off.

Cooking you Lemon and Lime Seabass

1. Pre-heat your air fryer to 380°f.

2. Cook the Lemon and Lime Seabass for 8-10 minutes or until golden brown.

Serving

Serve hot with Rice or Salad.

Oriental Seabass

Ingredients

4-6 Seabass Fillets

1 Clove of Garlic finely chopped

1 ½ inch piece of Ginger, grated

1 Teaspoon of Coriander

2 Tablespoons of Soy Sauce

1 Tablespoon of Sesame Oil

½ A Lime

Salt and Ground Black Pepper

Spring Onions finely chopped

1 Carrot, grated

Method

1. Mix the Garlic, Ginger, Coriander, Soy Sauce and Sesame Oil, a squeeze of Lime and a little Salt and Ground Black Pepper to taste.

2. Place the seabass in the oriental marinade and leave for at least an hour.

Cooking your Oriental Seabass

1. Pre-heat your air fryer to 380°f.

2. Cook the Oriental Seabass for 8-10 minutes or until the fillets begin to crisp.

Serving

Garnish with the Spring Onions and Grated Carrot, serve with Noodles and Soy Sauce.

Tomato and Herb Seabass

Ingredients

4-6 Seabass Fillets

1 Packet of Sun-dried Tomatoes chopped

1 Handful of Cherry Tomatoes chopped

½ Teaspoon of Basil

1 Teaspoon of Mixed Herbs

1 Tablespoon Tomato Puree

2 Cloves of Garlic finely chopped

1 White Onion finely chopped

½ Chicken Stock cube in 200ml water

Salt to taste

Method

1. Mix the Sun-Dried Tomatoes, Cherry Tomatoes and crush them with the back of a spoon.

2. Add the Mixed Herbs, Basil, Tomato Puree, Garlic, Salt and Chicken Stock.

3. Put the Seabass into the Tomato and Herb marinade and leave for at least 2 hours but preferably overnight.

Cooking your Tomato Herb Seabass

1. Pre-heat your air fryer to 360°f.

2. Lower the baking tray with the Seabass into your air fryer and cook for 18-20 minutes.

Serving

Serve hot with Rice or Salad and Pesto with a drizzle of the leftover Tomato and Herb Sauce Marinade.

Pan Fried Seabass with Chili Butter

Ingredients

4-6 Seabass fillets with the Skin still on.

100g Unsalted Butter

2 Tablespoon of Amarula Cream Liquor

1 Red Chili finely seeded and chopped

1 Green Chili finely seeded and chopped

½ A Lime

Olive Oil

Salt and Ground Black Pepper

Method

1. Lightly whisk the Butter, Chilies, Amarula Cream Liquor and a squeeze of Lime.

2. Season the Seabass Fillets with Salt and a little Ground Black Pepper.

Cooking your Pan Fried Seabass with Chili Butter

1. Put the baking tray in the air fryer and pre-heat to 380°f.

2. Place the seabass skin down on to the baking tray and air fry for 3-5 minutes, hold the fish down with a spatula to stop it curling.

3. Turn and cook for a further 2 minutes.

Serving

Serve hot with Salad or Rice.

Pan Fried Monkfish

Ingredients

2-4 Monkfish Fillets

Olive Oil

Salt and Ground Black Pepper to taste

1 Teaspoon of unsalted Butter

Half a Lemon

Method

1. Season the Monkfish with Salt and Ground Black Pepper and lightly spray with Olive Oil.

Cooking your Pan fried Monkfish

1. Put the baking tray into your air fryer and pre-heat your air fryer to 380°f.

2. Cook the Monkfish Fillets for 3-5 minutes and then turn for a further 2 minutes of cooking.

3. Add the Butter and a squeeze of Lemon and cook for a further 2 minutes.

Serving

Serve hot with Rice or Salad.

Air Fried Crab Cakes

Ingredients

400g Crabmeat, shredded

1 Cup of Seasoned Breadcrumbs

2 Teaspoons chopped Parsley

1 Teaspoon Paprika

1 Tablespoons of Mayonnaise

1 ½ Teaspoons of Mustard

Salt and Ground Black Pepper

Olive Oil

Method

1. Mix the shredded Crabmeat, Seasoned Breadcrumbs, Parsley, Paprika, Mayonnaise, Mustard, a little Salt and Ground Black Pepper to taste.
2. Using your hands form 4-6 'cakes' with the Crabmeat mix.

Cooking your Air fried Crab Cakes

1. Pre-heat your air fryer to 380°f.
2. Lightly spray your Crab Cakes with Olive Oil and air fry for 10-12 minutes or until golden brown, turning midway.

Serving

Serve hot with Salad.

Lobster Scampi with Homemade Scampi Sauce

Ingredients

300g Lobster meat cut into even sized large chunks

3 Cloves of Garlic finely chopped

1 Teaspoon of Italian Mixed Herbs

1 Teaspoon of Dijon Mustard

1 Tablespoon of Fresh Parsley finely chopped

1 Lemon

1 ½ Cups of White Wine

½ Cup of unsalted Butter

½ Cup Parmesan Cheese

Olive Oil

Salt and Ground Black Pepper to taste

Method

1. Cover the Lobster pieces with the Egg wash and roll them in the Seasoned Breadcrumb mix ensuring they are fully and evenly coated.

2. Press the Scampi pieces with your hands to make sure the Breadcrumbs are properly stuck.

3. Lightly spray the Scampi pieces with Olive Oil before air frying.

Cooking your Scampi Sauce

1. Put a small saucepan on medium heat and add a dash of Olive Oil.

2. Add the Garlic and cook for 1-2 minutes before mixing in the White Wine, Lemon Juice and Dijon Mustard, cook until the wine has reduced by half.

3. Add the Italian Mixed Herbs and Butter and reduce to a low heat.

4. Mix in the Chopped Parsley and a little Salt and Ground Black Pepper to taste.

5. Before serving add a sprinkling of Parmesan Cheese.

Cooking your Lobster Scampi

1. Pre-heat your air fryer to 380°f.

2. Air fry the Lobster Scampi for 6-8 minutes or until golden brown.

Serving

Serve hot with Scamp Sauce and a side Salad or Rice.

Butter Fired Scallops

Ingredients

400g Deshelled Scallops

30g Melted Butter

Salt and Ground Pepper to taste

Method

1. With a knife remove the side muscles from the Scallops, this is the bit on the side of the Scallop that secures it to the shell.

2. Season the Scallops with Salt and Pepper.

3. Mix the Butter with a little Salt and Pepper to taste and lightly coat the Scallops.

Cooking your Butter Fried Scallops

1. Pre-heat the air fryer to 380°f.

2. Place the Buttered Scallops in the air fryer basket and cook for 2 minutes before turning and cooking for a further minute or until golden.

Serving

Serve with Salad, a squeeze of Lemon Juice and Salt and Ground Black Pepper to taste.

Garlic and Ginger Scallops

Ingredients

400g Deshelled Scallops

3 Cloves of Garlic Finely chopped

1 Inch piece of Ginger grated

2 Tablespoons of Olive Oil

Salt and Ground Black Pepper to taste

Method

1. With a knife remove the side muscles from the scallop, this is the bit on the side of the Scallop that secures it to the shell.

2. Season the Scallops with Salt and Ground Black Pepper.

3. Mix the Olive Oil, Garlic, Ginger, Salt and Ground Black Pepper in a bowl.

4. Coat the Scallops in the mix allowing any excess Oil to drip back into the mix.

Cooking your Garlic and Ginger Scallops

1. Pre-heat the air fryer to 380°f.

2. Place the Scallops in the air fryer basket and cook for 2 minutes before turning and cooking for a further minute or until golden.

Serving

Serve with Salad, a squeeze of Lemon Juice and Salt and Ground Black Pepper to taste.

Vegetable dishes and Sides

Air Fried Bacon and Potato Rosties

Ingredients

2 Medium Russet Burbank or Maris Piper Potatoes coarsely grated.

3 Slices of Bacon

½ White Onion coarsely grated

Salt and Ground Pepper to taste

Method

1. Pre-heat your air fryer to 380°f and cook the Bacon slices for 3 minutes, remove from the air fryer and chop into small pieces and put to one side.

2. Soak the grated Potato in water for 2 minutes and rinse off to remove any excess starch. Squeeze the Potato to remove as much water as possible.

3. Add the Onion and Bacon to the Potato and mix thoroughly. Using your hands shape the Potato mix into 4-6 Rosties (burger shapes). Press firmly to make sure the Rosties are properly stuck.

4. Lightly spray the Rosties with Olive Oil before cooking.

Cooking your Air Fried Bacon and Potato Rosties

1. Pre-heat your air fryer to 380°f.

2. Place your Bacon and Potato Rosties in the air fryer basket and cook for 15 minutes or until golden brown, turning midway. Be sure not to overload your air fryer.

Serving

Serve hot with a fried Egg on top.

White Wine Batter Scallions

Ingredients

4 Bunches of Scallions, cleaned and trimmed

1 Cup of White Flour

¾ Cup of White Wine

Salt and Ground Black Pepper to taste

Olive Oil

Method

1. Mix the Flour, Salt and Ground Pepper in a bowl and pour in the White Wine, whisk until smooth.

2. Dip the Scallions into the mix, fully coating them. Allow any excess batter to drip back into the mix.

3. Lightly spray the Scallions with Olive Oil before cooking.

Cooking your White Wine Batter Scallions

1. Pre-heat your air fryer to 380°f.

2. Air fry the White Wine Batter Scallions for 3-5 minutes or until crisp and golden brown.

Serving

Serve hot with a sprinkling of Salt.

Perfect Beer Battered Onion Rings

Ingredients

1 Cup of Flour

¼ Teaspoon of Baking Soda

½ Teaspoon of Paprika

½ Teaspoon of Turmeric

1 Teaspoon of Salt

½ Teaspoon of Ground Black Pepper

½ Cup of Beer

1 Egg beaten well

1 large cup of Breadcrumbs

1 Large Sweet or Vidalia Onion peeled, sliced and separated into (approximately ½ inch) rings

Method

1. Start by mixing together the Flour, Baking Soda, Turmeric, Paprika, Salt, Ground Black Pepper and Beer in a bowl.

2. Add the beaten Egg and whisk until the mixture is smooth.

3. Put the Breadcrumbs in a separate bowl.

4. Dip the individual Onion Rings in the batter. Lift them out with a fork allowing any excess batter to drip off.

5. Place the batter covered Onion Rings into the Breadcrumb mix and cover with Breadcrumbs.

6. When removing the Onion Rings from the Breadcrumb mix apply light pressure with your hands to ensure the Breadcrumbs stay stuck.

7. Lightly spray the Onion Rings with Olive Oil on both sides.

Cooking your Onion Rings

1. Pre-heat your air fryer to 360°f.

2. Stack the Onion Rings in the air fryer in a disorderly fashion.

3. Air fry the Onion Rings for 10 minutes and turn before gently turning and frying for a further 5 minutes.

Serving

Serve hot with dips.

Corn on the Cob

Ingredients

4 Corns on the Cob

Butter and Salt to taste

Olive Oil

Method

1. Lightly Spray the Corns with Olive Oil.

Cooking your Corn on the Cob

1. Pre-heat your air fryer to 380°f.

2. Cook the Corn on the Cob for 4-6 minutes or until the edges start to blacken.

Serving

Serve hot with Butter and Salt.

Terrific Stuffed Peppers

Ingredients

4 Peppers 2x Red 2x Yellow cleaned, halved and deseeded.

80g Couscous

40g Feta Cheese, crumbled

1 Small handful of Pine Nuts, roasted

1 Teaspoon of Mixed Herbs

1 Packet of Sun-dried Tomatoes, chopped

Salt and Ground Black Pepper to taste

Olive Oil

1 Handful of Pomegranate Seeds

Method

1. Put the Couscous into a bowl and cover with 120ml boiling water and leave for 10 minutes.
2. After 10 minutes add the Feta Cheese, Pine Nuts, Mixed Herbs, Sun-Dried Tomatoes and a little Salt and Ground Black Pepper.
3. Spoon a pile of the Couscous mix into the Pepper halves.

Cooking your Terrific Stuffed Peppers

1. Pre-heat your air fryer to 360°f.
2. Place the Stuffed Peppers on the baking tray and air fry for 8-10 minutes.

Serving

Serve hot with a sprinkling of Pomegranate Seeds.

Broccoli and Parmesan Fritters

Ingredients

250g chopped Broccoli with stems peeled

½ Cup of Flour

1 Egg lightly beaten

30g or ¼ Cup of Parmesan

1 Clove of Garlic finely chopped

A sprinkling of Chili Flakes

½ Teaspoon of Salt

Ground Black Pepper to taste

Method

1. Boil or steam the Broccoli for 5 minutes before draining and allowing to cool. Lightly mash.
2. Mix the Flour, Parmesan, Garlic, Chili Flakes, Salt, Ground Black Pepper and Egg. Add the Broccoli and mix thoroughly.
3. Using your hands form this burger shapes from the mix, these will be your Fritters.
4. Lightly spray your Fritters with Olive Oil before cooking.

Cooking your Broccoli and Parmesan Fritters

1. Pre-heat your air fryer to 380°f.
2. Place the Broccoli and Parmesan Fritters in the air fryer and cook for 6 minutes or until crisp and golden brown turning midway.

Serving

Serve hot with a sprinkling of Salt and a squeeze of Lemon.

Honey Roasted Parsnips

Ingredients

3 Cups of Parsnips peeled and cut into chunky strips

1 Tablespoon of Olive Oil

¼ Teaspoon of Brown Sugar

Salt and Ground Black Pepper to taste

1 Tablespoon of Honey

Method

1. Mix the Olive Oil, Honey and Brown sugar together in a bowl, add the Parsnips and mix well, ensure all the Parsnips are thoroughly covered. Remove Parsnips and sprinkle on some Salt and Ground Black Pepper to taste.

Cooking your Honey Roasted Parsnips

1. Pre-heat your air fryer to 390°f.

2. Place the Parsnips haphazardly into the air fryer and cook for 14-16 minutes or until golden brown, tossing midway.

Serving

Serve hot. Honey Roasted Parsnips are great as a snack or a perfect side.

Honey Roasted Carrots

Ingredients

3 Cups of carrots cut into chunky strips

1 Tablespoon of Olive Oil

½ Teaspoon of Cumin

Salt and Ground Black Pepper to taste

1 Tablespoon of Honey

Method

1. Mix the Olive Oil, Honey and Cumin together in a bowl, add the Carrot and mix well, ensure all the Carrots are thoroughly covered. Remove Carrots and sprinkle on some Salt and Ground Black Pepper to taste.

Cooking your Honey Roasted Carrots

1. Pre-heat your air fryer to 390°f.

2. Place the Carrots haphazardly into the air fryer and cook for 12 minutes, toss midway.

Serving

Serve hot. Honey Roasted Carrots work great alongside most dishes.

Garlic Fried Asparagus

Ingredients

200g Asparagus

1 Clove of Garlic finely chopped and crushed

1 Tablespoon of Olive Oil

Salt and Ground Black Pepper to taste

Method

1. Mix the Olive Oil, Garlic in a bowl with a little Salt and Ground Black Pepper to taste.

2. Lightly coat the Asparagus with the Olive Oil and Garlic mix.

Cooking your Garlic Fried Asparagus

1. Pre-heat your air fryer to 360°.

2. Cook the Asparagus for 3-5 minutes.

Serving

Serve hot with Salmon or Steak

Roasted Peppers

Ingredients

Mixed Peppers deseeded and cut into quarters

2 Red Chilies finely chopped

1 Clove of Garlic finely chopped

1 Small White Onion finely chopped

1 Tablespoon of Olive Oil

Salt and Ground Black Pepper to taste

Method

1. Mix the chopped Peppers, Chilies, Garlic, Onion, Olive Oil and Salt and Ground Black Pepper to taste.

Cooking your Roasted Peppers

1. Pre-heat your air fryer to 380°f.

2. Place the mix into the baking tray and air fry for 20 minutes or until they begin to blacken at the edges.

Serving

Serve hot with Beef dishes.

Garlic Roasted Mushrooms

Ingredients

600g Creminis or Button Mushrooms sliced

2 Cloves of Garlic finely chopped

1 Teaspoon of Mixed Herbs

2 Tablespoons of White Wine

1 Tablespoon of Olive Oil

Method

1. Mix the Garlic, Mixed Herbs and Olive Oil in a bowl.

2. Keep your sliced Mushrooms to one side for now.

Cooking your Garlic Roasted Mushrooms

1. In the baking tray, air fry the Garlic and Herb mix for 1 ½ minutes on a low heat.

2. Stir in the Mushroom slices and increase the heat to 360°f for 25 minutes tossing regularly.

3. Add the White Wine and cook for a further 5 minutes.

Serving

Serve hot with beef or lamb dishes.

Rosemary and Garlic Roast Potatoes

Ingredients

500g Maris Piper Potatoes, peeled and halved

2 Cloves of Garlic finely chopped

1 Teaspoon of dried Rosemary

2 Tablespoons of Olive Oil

Salt and Ground Black Pepper to taste

Method

1. Place the Potatoes into a medium saucepan, cover with water and boil for 10 minutes

2. Whilst the Potatoes are boiling mix the Olive Oil, Garlic and Rosemary in a bowl.

3. Drain the Potatoes through a sieve and shake in order to 'roughen up' the outer Potato and then fully coat the Potatoes with the Garlic and Rosemary mix.

Cooking your Rosemary and Garlic Roast Potatoes

1. Pre-heat your air fryer to 390°f.

2. Air fry the Potatoes for 10 minutes or until golden brown.

Serving

Serve hot with a sprinkling of salt and Ground Black Pepper to taste.

Traditional Battered Fries

Ingredients

2 Medium Russet Burbank or Maris Piper Potatoes peeled and cut into chunky fries

1 Cup of Flour

2 Egg Whites

¼ Teaspoon of Fresh Ground Black Pepper

¼ Teaspoon Baking Powder

Salt to taste

Olive Oil

Method

1. Soak the Potato Fries in cold water for 30 minutes.

2. Mix the Flour, fresh ground Black Pepper and a little Salt (to taste) in a bowl.

3. Add the Egg Whites and whisk thoroughly until smooth and airy.

4. Remove the Potato Fries from the water and dry with kitchen towel.

Cooking your Traditional Battered Fries

1. Pre-heat your air fryer to 380°f.

2. Lightly spray your Fries with Olive Oil and place your Traditional Battered Fries haphazardly into the air fryer and cook for 20-22 minutes (tossing regularly) or until golden brown.

Serving

Serve hot with Salt and Malt Vinegar.

Beer Battered Fries

Ingredients

2 Medium Russet Burbank or Maris Piper Potatoes peeled and cut into chunky fries

1 Cup of Flour

1 Cup of Beer

½ Teaspoon of Cayenne Pepper

Salt to taste

Olive Oil

Method

1. Soak the Potato Fries in cold water for 30 minutes.

2. Mix the Flour, Cayenne Pepper and a little Salt (to taste) in a bowl.

3. Slowly pour the Beer into the mix, whisking throughout until smooth and airy.

4. Remove the Potato Fries from the water and dry with kitchen towel.

5. Dip the Fries individually into the Beer Batter allowing any excess to drip back into the bowl.

Cooking your Beer Battered Fries

1. Pre-heat your air fryer to 380°f.

2. Lightly spray your Fries with Olive Oil and place your Beer Battered Fries haphazardly into the air fryer and cook for 20-22 minutes (tossing regularly) or until golden brown.

Serving

Serve hot with Salt and Malt Vinegar.

Avocado Fries

Ingredients

1 Avocado halved, pitted and cut into ½ inch slices

2 Garlic Cloves finely chopped

½ Cup of Plain Flour

2 Eggs lightly beaten

½ Cup of Panko crumbs (available at Asian supermarkets)

2 Tablespoons of Olive Oil

½ Teaspoon of Cumin

½ Teaspoon of Cayenne Pepper

Salt and Ground Black Pepper to taste

Method

1. Mix the Olive Oil, Garlic, Cumin, Cayenne Pepper, and a little Salt and ground Black Pepper to taste.

2. Place the Flour, Eggs and Panko crumbs all into separate bowls.

3. Add the Avocado to the Olive Oil mix and fully coat the strips, when removing the Avocado allow any access mix to drip back into the bowl.

4. Coat the Avocado slices in the Flour ensuring they are evenly covered.

5. Brush the Avocado with the Egg wash and then dip them into the Panko crumb mix.

6. Lightly spray with Olive Oil before cooking.

Cooking your Avocado Fries

1. Pre-heat your air fryer to 380°f.

2. Cook the Avocado Fries for 20-25 minute or until golden brown and crisp.

Serving

Serve hot with a sprinkling of Salt.

Garlic and Ginger Potato Hash

Ingredients

1 Large Baking Potato, cleaned with skin on

3 Garlic Cloves finely chopped

1 inch piece of Ginger grated

2 Tablespoons of Olive Oil

Salt and Ground Black Pepper to taste

Method

1. Slice the Potatoes from top to bottom and lay the slices flat. Cut multiple slices from top to bottom and from left to right as to cut your Potato into rough cubes. Rinse the Potato cubes to remove any excess starch and then dry using kitchen towel.

2. Mix the Olive Oil, Garlic, Ginger with a little Salt and Ground Black Pepper to taste.

3. Add the Potato cubes to the mix and stir well to cover all of the cubes. Leave to marinade for 30 minutes.

Cooking your Garlic and Ginger Potato Hash

1. Pre-heat your air fryer to 360°f.

2. Toss your Garlic and Ginger Potato cubes into the air fryer and cook for 25 minutes or until crisp, toss throughout to ensure even cooking.

Serving

Serve hot, ideal with Salmon.

Air Fried Garlic Baked Potatoes

Ingredients

2 Russet Baking Potatoes

1 Clove of Garlic finely chopped

2 Tablespoon of Olive Oil

Salt and Ground Black Pepper

Method

1. Peirce the skin (with a fork) on both sides of the Potatoes.

2. Mix the Olive Oil, Garlic, Salt and Ground Black Pepper in a bowl and evenly coat the Potatoes in the mix.

Cooking your Air Fried Garlic Baked Potatoes

1. Pre-heat your air fryer to 390°f.

2. Air fry the Potatoes for 35-40 minutes.

Serving

Serve hot with butter

Garlic Roasted Sprouts

Ingredients

400g Brussel Sprouts sliced into halves

3 Cloves of Garlic finely chopped

1 Teaspoon of Mixed Herbs

1 Tablespoon of Olive Oil

Salt and Ground Black Pepper to taste

Method

1. Mix the Garlic, Mixed Herbs, Olive Oil, Salt and Ground Black Pepper in a bowl.

2. Add the Sprout halves and mix well ensuring they are evenly covered.

Cooking your Garlic Roasted Sprouts

1. Pre-heat your air fryer to 360°f.

2. Cook for 20-22 minutes tossing regularly.

Serving

Serve hot with Beef, Pork or Lamb dishes.

Honey Fried Sprouts

Ingredients

400g Brussel Sprouts sliced into halves

1 Clove of Garlic finely chopped

1 Tablespoon of Honey

1 Tablespoon of Olive Oil

1 Teaspoon Ground black Pepper

Salt to taste

Method

1. Mix the Garlic, Honey, Ground Black Pepper, Olive Oil and a little salt to taste.

2. Add the Sprouts and mix thoroughly ensuring the sprouts are fully coated.

Cooking your Honey Fried Sprouts

1. Pre-heat your air fryer to 360°f.

2. Cook for 20-22 minutes tossing regularly.

Serving

Serve hot with Beef or Lamb.

Air Fried Rice

Ingredients

175g Pilua Rice (Serves 2)

½ Red Onion finely chopped

1 Red Pepper chopped

1 Clove of Garlic finely chopped.

Salt and Ground Black Pepper to taste

1 Pot of Chicken Stock

400ml water

2 Tablespoons of Olive Oil

Method

1. Boil the water in a medium pan and add the stock cube.

2. Once the Stock Cube has fully dissolved, add the Rice along with some Salt and Ground Black Pepper to taste and stir thoroughly.

3. Cover the saucepan and boil for 10 minutes.

4. Take the pan off the boil and leave for a further 10 minutes.

5. Remove the Rice from the pan, place into a bowl and allow to cool.

Cooking your Air Fried Rice

1. Pre-heat your air fryer to 360°f.

2. Mix 1 tablespoon of Olive Oil, the Garlic, Onion and Pepper and pour into the air fryer for 1 ½ minutes.

3. Mix 1 Tablespoon of Olive Oil into the Rice and put the Rice in the air fryer for 10 minutes.

Serving

Serve with Chicken or Fish dishes.

Mash Potato Tots

Ingredients

2 Medium Russet Burbank or Maris Piper Potatoes peeled and halved

1 Teaspoon of Olive Oil

1 Teaspoon of Butter

Salt and Ground Black Pepper to taste

1 Cup of Seasoned Breadcrumbs

2 Eggs lightly beaten

Method

1. Boil the Potatoes in a medium saucepan for 18 minutes. Melt the Butter in the microwave whilst the Potatoes boil.

2. Drain the Potatoes and mash them along with the Olive Oil, Butter and some Salt and Ground Black Pepper to taste.

3. Shape the Potato into Tots, dip in the Egg Wash and Roll in the Seasoned Breadcrumb mix.

Cooking your Mash Potato Tots

1. Pre-heat your air fryer to 380°f.

2. Air fry the Mash Potato tots for 12 minutes tossing midway.

Serving

Serve hot with a sprinkling of Salt.

Seasoned Wedges

Ingredients

2 Large Russet Burbank or Maris Piper Potatoes

Salt and Ground Black Pepper to taste

Olive oil

Method

1. Cut the Potatoes into wedges.

2. In a Saucepan, boil the Potato Wedges on medium heat of 10 minutes.

3. Remove the Potato Wedges from the water and dry with kitchen towel.

4. Season the Wedges with plenty of Salt and ground Black Pepper.

5. Lightly spray with Olive Oil before cooking.

Cooking your Seasoned Wedges

1. Pre-heat your air fryer to 360°f.

2. Toss the Wedges into the air fryer and cook for 10-14 minutes, shake and continue to cook for a further 10 minutes.

Serving

Serve hot with dips, Sour Cream, Ketchup and Hot Sauce.

Sweet Potato Tots

Ingredients

2 Medium sized Sweet Potatoes

1 Teaspoon of Olive Oil

1 Teaspoon of Butter

Salt and Ground Black Pepper to taste

2 Eggs lightly beaten

1 Cup of Seasoned Breadcrumbs

Method

1. Boil the Sweet Potatoes in a medium saucepan for 12-14 minutes. Melt the Butter in the microwave whilst the Potatoes boil.

2. Drain the Sweet Potatoes and mash them along with the Olive Oil, Butter and some Salt and Ground Black Pepper to taste.

3. Shape the Sweet Potato into Tots.

4. Dip the Sweet Potato Tots into the Egg wash and roll in the Seasoned Breadcrumbs.

5. Lightly spray with Olive Oil before cooking.

Cooking your Sweet Potato Tots

1. Pre-heat your air fryer to 380°f.

2. Air fry the Sweet Potato tots for 12-15 minutes or until golden brown, tossing midway.

Serving

Serve hot with a sprinkling of Salt.

Sweet Potato Wedges

Ingredients

2 Medium Sweet Potatoes

Salt and Ground Black Pepper

Olive Oil

Method

1. Peel and cut the Sweet Potatoes into Wedges.

2. Season the Wedges with plenty of Salt and Ground Black Pepper.

3. Lightly spray with Olive Oil.

Cooking your Sweet Potato Wedges

1. Pre-heat your air fryer to 360°f.

2. Toss the Wedges into the air fryer and cook for 15 minutes, shake and continue to cook for a further 10 minutes.

Serving

Serve hot with a sprinkling of Salt.

Lemon Green Beans

Ingredients

300g Destemmed Green Beans

Half a fresh Lemon

Salt and Ground Black Pepper

Olive Oil

Cooking your Lemon Green Beans

1. Pre-heat your air fryer to 360°f.

2. Lightly spray the Green Beans with Olive Oil and put them into the air fryer along with a squeeze of Lemon Juice and a little Salt and Ground Black Pepper to taste.

3. Cook for 10-12 minutes.

Serving

Serve hot with a little Butter.

Fried Banana Chips

Ingredients

3 Bananas

1 Teaspoon of Salt

1 Teaspoon of Turmeric

1 Teaspoon of Chaat Masala

Water

Method

1. Mix the Salt and Turmeric in a bowl with water.

2. Evenly slice the Bananas and add them to the mix and leave for 5 minutes. This stops the Bananas from turning brown and will add a yellow colour when cooked.

3. Properly dry off the Banana slices with kitchen towel and lightly spray with Olive Oil.

Cooking your Banana Chips

1. Pre-heat your air fryer to 390°f.

2. Air fry the Banana slices for 15 minutes, tossing regularly.

3. Remove the cooked Banana slices and add Salt and Chaat Masala.

Serving

Serve hot or cold. For storage use an airtight container.

Crispy Seaweed

Ingredients

1 Bowl of Kale destemmed Kale Leaves

1 Teaspoon of Shrimp Powder (available at Asian supermarkets)

¼ Teaspoon of Sugar

¼ Teaspoon of Salt

Sesame Seeds

Method

1. Put the Kale leaves together and roll them up into a tight cylinder.

2. Finely slice the Kale in to thin strips.

3. Boil a saucepan of water on a medium heat. Toss the Kale strips into the water and blanch for 30 seconds.

4. Remove the Kale strips from the water and dry with kitchen towel.

5. Sprinkle with Salt, Sugar and Shrimp Powder.

Cooking your Crispy Seaweed

1. Pre-heat your air fryer to 340°.

2. Air fry your Crispy Seaweed for 45 seconds, tossing regularly.

Serving

Serve hot with Tuna Steak, Salad and a sprinkling of Sesame Seeds.

Roasted Garlic and Thyme Tomatoes

Ingredients

4 Roma Tomatoes, halved.

1 Clove of Garlic finely chopped

½ Teaspoon of dried Thyme

1 Tablespoon of Olive Oil

Salt and Ground Black Pepper to taste

Method

1. Scoop out most of the insides of the Tomato halves.

2. Mix the tomatoes, garlic, thyme an Olive Oil in a bowl with a little Salt and Ground Black Pepper to taste.

Cooking your Roasted Thyme Tomatoes

1. Pre-heat your air fryer to 380°f.

2. Air fry the Tomatoes cut side up for 15 minutes or until the edges crisp up and darken.

Serving

Serve hot with Ciabatta Bread.

Italian Style Bulgur Wheat Stuffed Tomatoes

Ingredients

4 Roma Tomatoes cut into halves

1 Cup of Bulgur Wheat

1 Teaspoon Italian Mixed Herbs

½ Teaspoon Oregano

1 Handful of chopped Spinach

Half a Lemon

Olive Oil

Method

1. Add 2 cups of water to a medium saucepan along with the bulgur wheat and bring to the boil before removing from the heat. Put a lid on the pan and leave for 10-12 minutes before pouring out any excess water.

2. To the Bulgur Wheat, add the Italian Mixed Herbs, Oregano, chopped Spinach, a squeeze of Lemon Juice and Salt and Ground Black Pepper to taste.

3. Scoop out the insides of the Tomatoes and spoon the Bulgur Wheat filling into the hollowed out Tomato halves.

4. Lightly spray with Olive Oil before cooking.

Cooking your Italian Style Bulgur Wheat Stuffed Tomatoes

1. Pre-heat your air fryer to 360°f.

2. Air fry the Tomato halves for 3 minutes before removing from the air fryer and stuffing with the Bulgur Wheat.

3. Return to the air fryer for a further 10-12 minutes.

Serving

Serve hot with Salad.

Deserts

Cinnamon Doughnuts

Ingredients

2 Large cups of plain White Flour

½ Cup of Sugar

½ Cup of Caster Sugar

1 Teaspoon of Baking Powder

2 Large Egg Yolks

50g Unsalted Butter

1 Tablespoon of melted unsalted Butter

1 Teaspoon of Salt

1 Teaspoon of Cinnamon

Method

1. In a large bowl press together the Butter and Sugar with the back of a wooden spoon.

2. Pour in the Egg yolks and stir until fully combined.

3. Sift the Flour into a separate bowl with the Baking Powder and Salt.

4. Add the Flour to the Egg, Butter and Sugar mix 1/3 at a time, mixing thoroughly throughout. Put the Dough in the fridge for 15 minutes.

5. Throw some Flour down on a clean surface, remove the Dough from the fridge and roll flat (around 1cm thick).

6. Using round pastry cutters (or a knife) cut the Dough into circles with smaller circles in the middle creating Doughnut shapes.

7. Brush the Doughnuts in the melted Butter before cooking.

8. Mix the Caster Sugar and Cinnamon in a bowl.

Cooking your Cinnamon Doughnuts

1. Pre-heat your air fryer to 360°f.

2. Air fry your Doughnuts for 8 minutes or until golden brown.

3. When your Doughnuts are cooked give them a second coating of melted Butter and then press the Doughnut into the Sugar and Cinnamon mix, ensuring the Doughnuts are fully coated.

Serving

Serve hot or cold.

Canadian Beaver Tails

Ingredients

9 Tablespoon of White Sugar

1 Tablespoon of Active Dry Yeast

½ Cup Warm (75°f) Water

4 Cups of plain Flour

2-¼ Cups of warm (75°f)Water

1 Teaspoon of Salt

1 Tablespoon of Lemon Juice

1 Teaspoon of Cinnamon

¼ Cup Olive Oil

Method

1. Place 1 tablespoon of Sugar and the Yeast into ½ cup of warm water and put to one side until the mix thickens and becomes creamy.

2. In a bowl mix the ¼ cup of Olive Oil, 2¼ cups of warm water, Lemon Juice, 5 tablespoons of Sugar and the Yeast mix.

3. Slowly add the Flour mixing thoroughly until you have smooth dough and place the dough in a buttered bowl to coat. Cover the bowl with a damp towel and leave to rest in a warm safe place for 1-½ hours.

4. Using your hands form 'dough balls' a little smaller than an egg and push flat to form ovals around 8mm thick and cut out a small hole from the centre of the oval.

5. Lightly spray with Olive Oil before cooking.

Cooking your Canadian Beavertail Doughnuts

1. Pre-heat your air fryer to 380°f.

2. Lay your Canadian Beavertail Doughnuts flat in the air frying basket and cook for 2-3 minutes turning midway. Be careful not to overload your air fryer.

Serving

Serve hot with a sprinkling of Sugar and Cinnamon mix.

Banana Fritters

Ingredients

2 Bananas cut into halves

1 Cup of Flour

2 Eggs

¼ cup of Milk

2 Tablespoons of Icing Sugar

Olive Oil

Method

1. In a bowl whisk the Flour, Eggs, Milk and Icing Sugar until smooth.

2. Generously coat the Banana halves in the batter mix and lightly spray with Olive Oil.

Cooking your Banana Fritters

1. Pre-heat your air feyer to 360°f.

2. Line the air fryer basket with foil and cook the Banana Fritters for 3 minutes or until golden brown. Turn midway.

Serving

Serve hot with Ice-cream.

Pineapple Fritters

Ingredients

1 Pack/tin of Pineapple Rings

1 Cup of Flour

2 Eggs

¼ cup of Milk

2 Tablespoons of Icing Sugar

Method

1. In a bowl whisk the Flour, Eggs, Milk and Icing Sugar until smooth.

2. Generously coat the Pineapple Rings in the batter mix and lightly spray with Olive Oil.

Cooking you Pineapple Fritter

1. Pre-heat your air feyer to 360°f.

2. Line the air fryer basket with foil and cook the Pineapple Fritters for 3 minutes or until golden brown. Turn midway.

Serving

Serve hot with Ice-cream.

Battered Melon Balls

Ingredients

1 Melon, balled

1 Cup of Flour

2 Eggs

¼ cup of Milk

2 Tablespoons of Icing Sugar

Method

1. In a bowl whisk the Flour, Eggs, Milk and Icing Sugar until smooth.

2. Generously coat the Melon balls in the batter mix and lightly spray with Olive Oil.

Cooking you Melon Balls

1. Pre-heat your air feyer to 360°f.

2. Line the air fryer basket with foil and cook the Melon Balls for 3 minutes or until golden brown. Turn midway.

Serving

Serve hot with Ice-cream.

Battered 'Mars' Bar

Ingredients

2 Mars bars or Chocolate bar of your choice

1 Cup of Flour

2 Eggs

¼ cup of Milk

2 Tablespoons of Icing Sugar

Olive Oil

Method

1. In a bowl whisk the Flour, Eggs, Milk and Icing Sugar until smooth.

2. Generously coat the Chocolate pieces in the batter mix and lightly spray with Olive Oil.

Cooking your Battered 'Mars' Bar

1. Pre-heat your air feyer to 360°f.

2. Line the air fryer basket with foil and cook the Battered 'Mars' Bars for 3 minutes or until golden brown. Turn midway.

Serving

Serve hot with Ice-cream.

Classic Jam Doughnuts

Ingredients

9 Tablespoon of White Sugar

1 Tablespoon of Active Dry Yeast

½ Cup Warm (75°f) Water

4 Cups of plain Flour

2-¼ Cups of warm (75°f)Water

1 Teaspoon of Salt

1 ½ Teaspoons of Vanilla Extract

1 Teaspoon of Cinnamon

¼ Cup Olive Oil

4 Tablespoons of Jam, Apple & Raspberry or Strawberry.

1 Tablespoon of Rum

Icing Sugar

Method

1. Place 1 tablespoon of Sugar and the Yeast into ½ cup of warm water and put to one side until the mix thickens and becomes creamy.

2. In a bowl mix the ¼ cup of Olive Oil, 2¼ cups of warm water, 5 tablespoons of Sugar and the yeast mix.

3. Slowly add the Flour mixing thoroughly until you have smooth Dough and place the Dough in a buttered bowl to coat. Cover the bowl with a damp towel and leave to rest in a warm safe place for 1-½ hours.

4. Once the Dough had doubled in size prepare the doughnut filling by mixing the Jam with the Rum.

5. Using your hands shape small egg sized ball of Dough and then roll them flat (2cm thick).

6. Spoon some Jam into the centre of the dough and fold over the dough to cover. Be sure that the Jam is properly covered and fully contained within the Doughnut.

Cooking your Classic Jam Doughnuts

1. Pre-heat your air fryer to 380°f.

2. Air fry your Classic Jam Doughnuts for 3-4 minutes or until golden brown. Turn midway.

Serving

Serve with a sprinkling of Icing Sugar. Allow to cool before serving, the Jam inside will be piping hot!

So Chocolate Cake

Ingredients

1 Cup of Flour

1 Cup Brown Sugar

½ Cup Unsweetened Cocoa Powder

1 Teaspoon of Baking Powder

½ Teaspoon of Salt

1 Large Egg lightly beaten

½ Cup of Milk

½ A cup of warm Water (add coffee as per your taste)

1 Teaspoon of Vanilla Essence

¼ Teaspoon Nutmeg

¼ Teaspoon Cinnamon

¼ Cup of Vegetable Oil

Method

1. In a bowl mix the Flour Baking Soda, Salt, Nutmeg, Cinnamon, Cocoa Powder and Sugar.

2. First add the Milk then Egg and then Olive Oil and Vanilla extract to the mix, stir thoroughly.

3. Lastly add the warm water and stir until the mixture is smooth.

Cooking your So Chocolate Cake

1. Pre-heat your air fryer to 360°f.

2. Pour the So Chocolate Cake mix into the baking tray, cover with foil and pierce air holes in the foil. Lower the baking tray into the air fryer and cook for 30-35 minutes.

Serving

Serve hot with Ice-cream.

Caramel Popcorn

Ingredients

Corn Kernels

4 Tablespoons of Brown Sugar

2 Tablespoons of Butter

Method (Caramel)

1. Whilst the Corn Kernels are cooking melt the butter in a medium saucepan on medium and add the Sugar. Stir continuously to stop any burning.

2. Once the Sugar and Butter begin to caramelise, toss in the Popcorn (fresh from the air fryer). Shake the Popcorn in the Caramel and evenly coat before removing from the saucepan.

Cooking your Caramel Popcorn

1. Pre-heat your air fryer to 390°f.

2. Air fry the Corn Kernels for 5-6 minutes, keep an eye on them!

Serving

Serve warm, be careful as the Caramel will be hot!

Profiteroles

Ingredients

Profiteroles

200g Plain Flour

100g Butter

5 Large Eggs

300ml Water

Olive Oil

Cream Filling

2 Teaspoons of Vanilla Essence

3 Teaspoons of Icing Sugar

300ml Whipped Cream

Chocolate Sauce

120 Dark Chocolate broken into chunks

2 Tablespoons of Whipped Cream

50g Butter

Method

Profiteroles

1. Put the Water into a medium saucepan on a medium heat, add the Butter and stir until melted.

2. Add the Flour to the mix a bit at a time whilst stirring until a Dough forms. Remove from the heat, place the Dough in a bowl and mix in the Eggs until you have a smooth mixture.

3. Using your hands form Profiterole shapes.

4. Lightly Spray with Olive Oil before cooking.

Cream Filling

1. Whisk together the 300ml Whipped Cream, Vanilla Essence and Icing Sugar until thick and creamy.

Chocolate Sauce

1. Boil some water in a saucepan and place a glass bowl on the top. Put the Chocolate pieces into the glass bowl and mix until melted.

2. Add the Whipped cream and Butter to the melted Chocolate.

Cooking your Profiteroles

1. Pre-heat your air fryer to 360°f.

2. Cook your Profiteroles for 9-11 minutes or until golden brown, turning regularly.

Serving

Spoon or pipe some of the Cream Filling into the Profiteroles and top with Chocolate Sauce.

Printed in Great Britain
by Amazon